On and Off the Bus

Written by
Stephen Rickard

Illustrated by
Veronica Montoya

Ransom

"Let us run to the big red bus. It has a big ten on it," Mum tells Dad and Nell. "Let us get on the bus."

Mum, Dad and Nell get on the bus.

Dad gets the bus tickets.
Dad has the tickets in his pocket.

Mum, Dad and Nell sit
at the top of the bus.

At the top of the hill,
Dad taps the bell.

Mum, Dad and Nell get off the bus.

Mum has a map.

"Let us go and sit in the sun," Mum tells Dad and Nell.

Mum, Dad and Nell sit in the sun.

At sunset, Mum, Dad and Nell go to get the bus.

Nell has a nap on the bus.